Introduction

For those who want to elevate their holiday meals, this book brings you a selection of elegant and sophisticated recipes that are sure to impress. From exquisite appetizers to decadent desserts, each dish is crafted to turn your Christmas table into a feast of flavors. Let's make your holiday dining truly special with recipes that celebrate the art of fine cooking!

Table of content

Table of content

Herb-Crusted Beef Tenderloin

Ingredients

Beef tenderloin
Dijon mustard
Dried thyme
Dried rosemary
Dried sage
Olive oil
Salt and pepper

Instruction

1. Preheat oven to 425°F (220°C).
2. Remove tenderloin from refrigerator and let stand for 30 minutes to reach room temperature.
3. In a small bowl, combine mustard, thyme, rosemary, sage, olive oil, salt, and pepper. Rub evenly over tenderloin.
4. Place tenderloin on a roasting rack set in a roasting pan.
5. Roast for 20-25 minutes, or until the internal temperature reaches 135°F (57°C) for medium-rare.

Rating

Rating: 4/5

Cooking time

Cooking time: 20-25 minutes

Tips

Use high-quality Brie cheese for a rich and creamy flavor.
Don't overstuff the crescent rolls, as they will burst open during baking.
Sprinkle the sugar and cinnamon generously for a sweet and crunchy topping.

Garlic Butter Lobster Tails

Ingredients

Lobster tails
Butter
Garlic
Olive oil
Lemon juice
Salt and pepper

Instruction

1. Heat olive oil in a large skillet over medium-high heat.
2. Add lobster tails and cook for 2-3 minutes per side, or until browned.
3. Add butter, garlic, lemon juice, salt, and pepper to the skillet.
4. Baste lobster tails with the butter mixture for 1-2 minutes, or until cooked through.
5. Serve immediately with additional lemon juice if desired.

Rating

Rating: 4/5

Cooking time

Cooking time: 5 minutes

Tips

Use fresh ingredients for the best flavor.
Don't overstuff the mushrooms, or they will burst in the oven.
Bake until the mushrooms are tender and the filling is hot and bubbly.

Roasted Duck with Cherry Sauce

Ingredients

Duck
Cherries
Port wine
Sugar
Spices
Herbs

Instruction

1. Season the duck with salt and pepper, and roast in a preheated oven until golden brown.
2. Reduce the oven temperature and roast the duck until cooked through.
3. While the duck is roasting, make the cherry sauce by simmering cherries, port wine, sugar, and spices in a saucepan until thickened.
4. Remove the duck from the oven and let it rest for 10 minutes before carving.
5. Serve the roasted duck with the cherry sauce.

Rating

Rating: 4/5

Cooking time

Cooking time: 2 hours

Tips

Roast or steam your pumpkin until tender and then puree it.
In a food processor, combine the pumpkin puree, chickpeas, tahini, lemon juice, cumin, salt, and pepper. Blend until smooth.
Refrigerate the hummus for at least 30 minutes before serving.

Truffle Risotto with Wild Mushrooms

Ingredients

Carnaroli rice
Olive oil
Onion
Garlic
Wild mushrooms (such as chanterelles, shiitake, or oyster mushrooms)
Dry white wine
Chicken or vegetable stock
Truffle oil
Parmesan cheese
Salt and pepper

Instruction

1. Sauté onion and garlic in olive oil until softened.
2. Add wild mushrooms and cook until golden brown.
3. Stir in Carnaroli rice and cook for 1 minute.
4. Add white wine and let it reduce.
5. Gradually add stock while stirring constantly until rice is cooked al dente. Stir in truffle oil, Parmesan cheese, salt, and pepper.

Rating

Rating: 5/5

Cooking time

Cooking time: 30 minutes

Tips

Use fresh spinach for the best flavor.
Add a pinch of red pepper flakes for a little heat.
Serve with your favorite chips, crackers, or vegetables.

Salmon en Croûte with Spinach

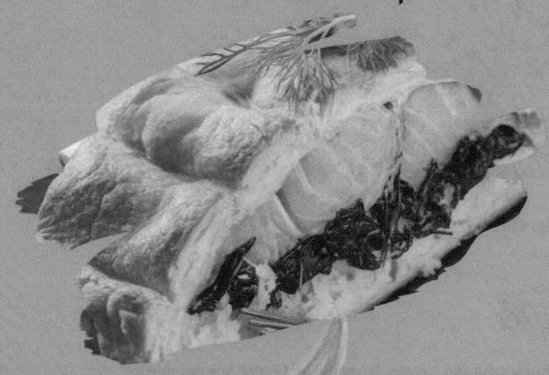

Ingredients

Salmon fillets
Puff pastry
Dijon mustard
Spinach
Cream cheese
Parmesan cheese
Salt and pepper
Egg wash

Instruction

1. Preheat oven to 400°F (200°C).
2. Season salmon fillets with salt and pepper, and spread with Dijon mustard.
3. Sauté spinach and combine with cream cheese and Parmesan cheese.
4. Unroll puff pastry and spread the spinach mixture in the center. Place the salmon fillets on top and fold the pastry over, sealing the edges.
5. Brush with egg wash and bake for 20-25 minutes, or until the pastry is golden brown.

Rating

Rating: 4.5/5

Cooking time

Cooking time: 20-25 minutes

Tips

Don't overcook the squash. It should be tender but not mushy.
Use a blender or food processor to puree the soup until smooth.
Garnish the soup with a dollop of sour cream or a sprinkle of toasted nuts.

Balsamic Glazed Brussels Sprouts with Pecans

Ingredients

Brussels sprouts
Olive oil
Balsamic vinegar
Maple syrup
Dijon mustard
Salt
Pepper
Pecans

Instruction

1. Trim and halve Brussels sprouts. Toss with olive oil, salt, and pepper.
2. Roast at 400°F for 20 minutes, or until tender.
3. Whisk together balsamic vinegar, maple syrup, and Dijon mustard in a small saucepan. Bring to a simmer and cook until thickened, about 5 minutes.
4. Pour glaze over roasted Brussels sprouts and toss to coat.
5. Sprinkle with pecans and serve.

Rating

Rating: 4/5

Cooking time

Cooking time: 25 minutes

Tips

Try topping these casseroles with toasted marshmallows for a sweet and crunchy treat.

For a creamy casserole, add a dollop of whipped cream on top.

Don't overmix the sweet potato mixture, as this will make the casseroles tough.

Coq au Vin (Chicken in Red Wine)

Ingredients

Chicken, cut into pieces
Bacon, chopped
Onions, chopped
Carrots, chopped
Celery, chopped
Garlic, minced
Red wine
Chicken broth
Herbs, such as thyme, rosemary, and bay leaves
Salt and pepper

Instruction

1. Brown chicken and bacon in a large pot.
2. Add vegetables and sauté until softened.
3. Add red wine and cook until reduced by half.
4. Add chicken broth, herbs, salt, and pepper.
5. Simmer until chicken is tender.

Rating

Rating: 4/5

Cooking time

Cooking time: 2 hours

Tips

Trim asparagus spears before wrapping with bacon for a more even cook.
Bake on a lightly greased baking sheet to prevent sticking.
Don't overcook the bacon, as it will become tough.

Lobster Bisque with Cognac

Ingredients

Lobster shells
Butter
Onion, diced
Celery, diced
Carrot, diced
Tomato paste
Cognac
Fish stock
Heavy cream
Cayenne pepper
Paprika
Salt, to taste

Instruction

1. Sauté lobster shells in butter until fragrant.
2. Add onion, celery, carrot, and tomato paste; cook until softened.
3. Deglaze pan with cognac and let alcohol reduce.
4. Add fish stock, heavy cream, cayenne pepper, paprika, and salt; simmer for 15 minutes.
5. Strain bisque and discard solids.

Rating

Rating: 4/5

Cooking time

Cooking time: 30 minutes

Tips

Start with a variety: Include at least three types of cheese, three charcuterie meats, and a selection of crackers, fruit, nuts, and olives.
Arrange visually: Group similar items together and fill in empty spaces to create a balanced and visually appealing board.
Add some greenery: Scatter fresh herbs or edible flowers around the board for a touch of freshness and color.

Stuffed Acorn Squash with Quinoa and Cranberries

Ingredients

Acorn squash
Quinoa
Cranberries
Onion
Celery
Carrots
Olive oil
Salt
Pepper
Maple syrup
Pecans

Instruction

1. Preheat oven to 400°F (200°C). Cut squash in half lengthwise; scoop out seeds and pulp. Place squash halves cut-side up on a baking sheet.
2. Cook quinoa according to package directions.
3. Sauté onion, celery, and carrots in olive oil until softened. Stir in cranberries, maple syrup, salt, and pepper.
4. Fill squash halves with quinoa mixture. Sprinkle with pecans.
5. Bake 35-45 minutes, or until squash is tender and quinoa is cooked through.

Rating

Rating: 4/5

Cooking time

Cooking time: 35-45 minutes

Tips

For smoother deviled eggs, press the yolks through a fine-mesh sieve before mixing.
Add a dollop of sour cream or Greek yogurt to the yolk mixture for extra creaminess.
For a smoky flavor, cook the bacon until crispy and then crumble it over the deviled eggs.

Pork Tenderloin with Apple Cider Reduction

Ingredients

Pork tenderloin
Olive oil
Salt and pepper
Apple cider
Dijon mustard
Honey
Brown sugar

Instruction

1. Season pork tenderloin with salt and pepper.
2. Heat olive oil in a skillet and brown pork on all sides.
3. Remove pork and set aside.
4. In the same skillet, combine apple cider, Dijon mustard, honey, and brown sugar.
5. Bring to a boil and reduce heat. Simmer for 5-7 minutes or until sauce thickens.

Rating

Rating: 4/5

Cooking time

Cooking time: 10-12 minutes

Tips

Roast sweet potatoes thoroughly: Ensure they are tender and cooked through for optimal flavor and texture.

Sauté veggies until softened: Allow the onion and bell pepper to caramelize slightly for a sweeter, more intense taste.

Layer filling generously: Spread the sweet potato mixture evenly over the tortillas to prevent empty or overstuffed sections.

Chateaubriand with Bearnaise Sauce

Ingredients

Chateaubriand:
Beef tenderloin roast
Olive oil
Salt and pepper
Bearnaise Sauce:
Unsalted butter
Shallots
Tarragon
White wine vinegar
Egg yolks

Instruction

1. Preheat oven to 400°F (200°C).
2. Season beef with salt and pepper, then sear in hot olive oil.
3. Roast for 15-20 minutes, or until internal temperature reaches 135°F (57°C) for medium-rare.
4. Let rest for 10 minutes before slicing.
5. Make the Bearnaise sauce by whisking together melted butter, shallots, tarragon, vinegar, and egg yolks.

Rating

Rating: 4/5

Cooking time

Cooking time: 35-40 minutes

Tips

Preheat oven to 450°F (230°C) for initial high-temperature roasting.
Massage a flavorful herb mixture of rosemary, sage, thyme, and olive oil into the turkey skin.
Pour chicken broth into the roasting pan to keep the turkey moist during cooking.

Duck Confit with Orange Marmalade

Ingredients

Duck legs
Salt
Black pepper
Thyme
Rosemary
Orange marmalade
Port wine (optional)

Instruction

1. Season duck legs generously with salt, pepper, thyme, and rosemary.
2. Place the legs in a baking dish and cover with orange marmalade.
3. Add port wine if desired.
4. Cook in a preheated oven at 160°C (320°F) for 3-4 hours, or until tender.
5. Remove the legs from the oven and let them rest for 10 minutes before serving.

Rating

Rating: 4/5

Cooking time

Cooking time: 3-4 hours

Tips

Score the ham for even glaze absorption.
Cover the ham for initial roasting to prevent burning.
Monitor the internal temperature to ensure doneness.

Elegant Beef Wellington

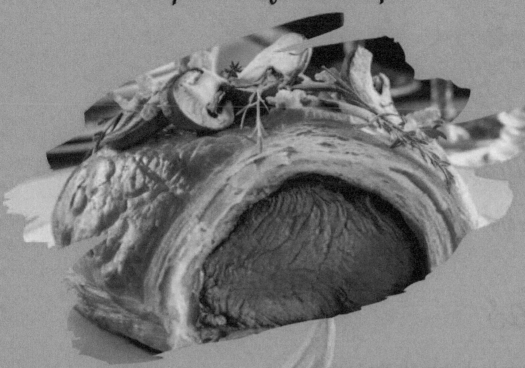

Ingredients

1 beef tenderloin
1 pound mushrooms
1/2 onion
1/4 cup parsley
1/4 cup thyme
1/2 cup Madeira wine
1/2 cup beef broth
1 tablespoon Worcestershire sauce
1/2 teaspoon salt
1/4 teaspoon black pepper
1 puff pastry sheet

Instruction

1. Preheat oven to 400°F (200°C).
2. Season beef with salt and pepper, then sear on all sides in a pan.
3. Chop mushrooms, onion, parsley, and thyme and sauté in a pan. Deglaze with Madeira wine and beef broth.
4. Spread mushroom mixture evenly over seared beef and wrap in puff pastry.
5. Bake for 30-35 minutes, or until golden brown and cooked through.

Rating

Rating: 4/5

Cooking time

Cooking time: 30-35 minutes

Tips

Use a whole chicken for the best flavor.
Preheat the oven to 400°F (200°C) for even cooking.
Let the chicken rest for 15 minutes before carving to allow the juices to redistribute.

Pan-Seared Scallops with Lemon Butter

Ingredients

Large scallops
Salt and pepper
Olive oil
Butter
Lemon juice
Parsley

Instruction

1. Season scallops with salt and pepper.
2. Heat olive oil in a skillet over medium-high heat.
3. Sear scallops for 2-3 minutes per side, or until golden brown.
4. Add butter and lemon juice to the skillet and baste the scallops.
5. Cook for an additional 1-2 minutes, or until the scallops are cooked through.

Rating

Rating: 4/5

Cooking time

Cooking time: 3-5 minutes

Tips

Brine the turkey breast for at least 12 hours, but no more than 24 hours.
Remove the turkey breast from the brine and pat dry before roasting.
Roast the turkey breast until the internal temperature reaches 165 degrees F.

Butternut Squash and Sage Ravioli

Ingredients

Butternut squash
Onion
Garlic
Fresh sage
Heavy cream
Parmesan cheese
Ravioli dough

Instruction

1. Roast and puree the butternut squash.
2. Sauté onion, garlic, and sage in butter.
3. Combine squash puree with sautéed mixture, heavy cream, and Parmesan cheese.
4. Roll out ravioli dough and fill with squash mixture.
5. Cook ravioli in boiling water until tender.

Rating

Rating: 4/5

Cooking time

Cooking time: 3-4 minutes

Tips

Prep the vegetables: Chop the mushrooms, onion, and garlic. Wilt the spinach by sautéing it in a pan until it reduces in size.

Make the filling: Sauté the mushrooms, onion, and garlic in olive oil. Add the wilted spinach, breadcrumbs, and feta cheese. Season with salt and pepper.

Assemble the Wellington: Roll out the puff pastry and spread the mushroom mixture evenly over the bottom half. Fold the top half of the pastry over the filling and seal the edges. Bake at 400°F (200°C) for 30-40 minutes, or until golden brown.

Caramelized Shallot and Goat Cheese Tart

Ingredients

1 (9inch) unbaked pie crust
2 cups thinly sliced shallots
1 tablespoon olive oil
1 tablespoon balsamic vinegar
1/2 cup crumbled goat cheese
1/4 cup heavy cream
1 egg
1/4 teaspoon salt
1/4 teaspoon black pepper

Instruction

1. Preheat oven to 425°F (220°C).
2. Sauté shallots in olive oil until caramelized. Add balsamic vinegar and cook until reduced.
3. In a bowl, whisk together goat cheese, heavy cream, egg, salt, and pepper.
4. Pour shallot mixture into pie crust and top with goat cheese mixture.
5. Bake for 15-20 minutes, or until crust is golden brown and filling is set.

Rating

Rating: 5/5

Cooking time

Cooking time: 15-20 minutes

Tips

To enhance flavor, season Cornish hens with a spice blend of kosher salt, black pepper, smoked paprika, and more.
For even cooking, let hens rest at room temperature before roasting.
Ensure hens are cooked thoroughly by roasting until internal temperature reaches 165°F.

Roasted Vegetable and Feta Salad

Ingredients

Bell peppers
Zucchini
Onion
Cherry tomatoes
Olive oil
Salt
Pepper
Feta cheese
Fresh parsley

Instruction

1. Preheat oven to 425°F (220°C).
2. Toss bell peppers, zucchini, onion, and cherry tomatoes with olive oil, salt, and pepper.
3. Spread vegetables on a baking sheet and roast for 20-25 minutes, or until tender and slightly browned.
4. Crumble feta cheese over the roasted vegetables.
5. Garnish with fresh parsley and serve warm.

Rating

Rating: 4/5

Cooking time

Cooking time: 20-25 minutes

Tips

For even cooking, cut vegetables into uniform sizes.
Don't overcrowd the roasting pan, or the vegetables will steam instead of roast.
Glaze the vegetables with honey during the last 5 minutes of cooking for a perfect balance of sweetness and caramelization.

Wild Mushroom Tart with Thyme

Ingredients

Puff pastry
Olive oil
Wild mushrooms
Shallots
Garlic
Thyme
Parmesan cheese
Salt and pepper

Instruction

1. Preheat oven to 400°F (200°C). Line a baking sheet with parchment paper.
2. In a large skillet, heat olive oil over medium heat. Add mushrooms, shallots, and garlic and cook until softened.
3. Stir in thyme, Parmesan cheese, salt, and pepper. Cook for 1 minute more.
4. Unfold puff pastry sheet on the prepared baking sheet. Spread mushroom mixture over the pastry, leaving a 1-inch border.
5. Bake for 20-25 minutes, or until the pastry is golden brown and the mushrooms are cooked through.

Rating

Rating: 4/5

Cooking time

Cooking time: 20-25 minutes

Tips

Preheat oven to 400°F.
Brush squash with olive oil, salt, and pepper before baking.
Stuff squash with cooked quinoa mixture and bake for 40-45 minutes.

Cranberry and Pistachio Baked Brie

Ingredients

Brie cheese
Cranberry sauce
Pistachios
Puff pastry

Instruction

1. Preheat oven to 375°F (190°C).
2. Roll out puff pastry and cut a circle large enough to wrap around the brie.
3. Place brie in the center of the pastry and top with cranberry sauce and pistachios.
4. Wrap the pastry around the brie, pressing the edges to seal.
5. Bake for 20-25 minutes, or until the pastry is golden brown and the brie is melted and bubbly.

Rating

Rating: 4/5

Cooking time

Cooking time: 20-25 minutes

Tips

To save time, preheat the grill while preparing the glaze.
For a crispier skin, grill the salmon skin-side down.
Don't overcook the salmon; it should be cooked through but still moist.

Spiced Pear and Gorgonzola Salad

Ingredients

Bosc pears
Olive oil
Spices (cinnamon, nutmeg, ginger)
Mixed greens
Gorgonzola cheese
Honey
Walnuts
Balsamic vinegar

Instruction

1. Cut pears into slices and toss with olive oil, spices, and a drizzle of honey.
2. Grill or roast pears until caramelized and tender.
3. Arrange mixed greens on plates and top with pears, crumbled Gorgonzola, chopped walnuts, and a drizzle of balsamic vinegar.
4. Finish with an extra drizzle of honey for sweetness.
5. Serve immediately.

Rating

Rating: 4/5

Cooking time

Cooking time: 15 minutes

Tips

Brown ribs thoroughly for maximum flavor.
Simmer red wine until reduced to enhance its richness.
Braise for 2-3 hours to ensure tender, fall-off-the-bone ribs.

Lamb Chops with Rosemary and Garlic

Ingredients

Lamb chops
Rosemary
Garlic
Olive oil
Salt
Pepper

Instruction

1. Season lamb chops with salt and pepper.
2. Heat olive oil in a skillet over medium heat.
3. Add lamb chops and sear for 2-3 minutes per side.
4. Add rosemary and garlic to the skillet.
5. Cook until rosemary is fragrant and garlic is golden brown.

Rating

Rating: 4/5

Cooking time

Cooking time: 10 minutes

Tips

For creamier potatoes, use a potato ricer instead of a masher.
Add a splash of cream or sour cream to the milk for extra richness.
Garnish with chopped chives or parsley for a pop of color.

Saffron and Lobster Risotto

Ingredients

Arborio rice
Saffron threads
Onion
Garlic
Dry white wine
Lobster stock
Lobster meat
Parmesan cheese
Butter

Instruction

1. Sauté onion and garlic in butter until softened.
2. Add rice and stir until translucent.
3. Add wine and simmer until absorbed.
4. Gradually stir in lobster stock until rice is al dente.
5. Fold in lobster meat, saffron-infused butter, and Parmesan cheese.

Rating

Rating: 5/5

Cooking time

Cooking time: 30 minutes

Tips

Trim green beans carefully: Cut off both ends of the beans to ensure they're tender and evenly cooked.

Toast almonds until golden: Keep a close eye on the almonds to prevent burning, which can add bitterness.

Season to taste: Add salt and pepper gradually, adjusting to your desired flavor.

Braised Short Ribs with Red Wine

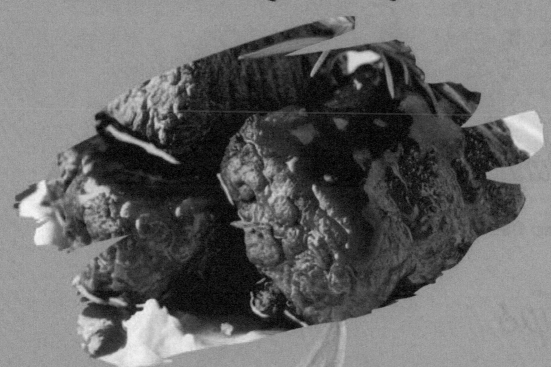

Ingredients

Short ribs
Red wine
Beef broth
Vegetables (onions, carrots, celery)
Garlic
Thyme
Rosemary
Bay leaves

Instruction

1. Season the short ribs with salt and pepper and brown them in a large pot over medium-high heat.
2. Remove the short ribs from the pot and add the vegetables, garlic, thyme, rosemary, and bay leaves to the pot.
3. Cook the vegetables for 5-7 minutes until softened, then add the red wine and beef broth to the pot.
4. Bring the mixture to a boil, then reduce heat to low and simmer for 2-3 hours, or until the short ribs are fall-off-the-bone tender.
5. Serve the short ribs with the sauce and your favorite sides.

Rating

Rating: 4/5

Cooking time

Cooking time: 2-3 hours

Tips

For a creamier texture, use a potato masher instead of a food processor to mash the potatoes.
Add a pinch of salt to the sweet potato mixture to enhance the flavors.
If you don't have marshmallows, you can top the casserole with a crunchy pecan topping made from butter, brown sugar, and chopped pecans.

Herbed Couscous with Pomegranate

Ingredients

Couscous
Water
Vegetable broth
Olive oil
Herbs (thyme, oregano, rosemary)
Salt
Pepper
Pomegranate seeds
Pistachios

Instruction

1. Bring water and vegetable broth to a boil in a saucepan.
2. Add couscous and remove from heat. Cover and let stand for 5 minutes.
3. Fluff couscous with a fork and drizzle with olive oil.
4. Stir in herbs, salt, and pepper.
5. Top with pomegranate seeds and pistachios.

Rating

Rating: 4/5

Cooking time

Cooking time: 5 minutes

Tips

Trim and halve Brussels sprouts.
Toss with olive oil, salt, and pepper.
Add minced garlic and roast for 20 minutes.

Caramelized Fennel and Citrus Salad

Ingredients

Fennel bulbs
Oranges
Grapefruits
Lemons
Sugar
Olive oil
Salt
Pepper

Instruction

1. Preheat oven to 400°F (200°C).
2. Trim and slice the fennel bulbs into thin wedges.
3. Cut the oranges, grapefruits, and lemons into segments.
4. Toss the fennel, citrus segments, sugar, olive oil, salt, and pepper in a large bowl.
5. Roast for 20-25 minutes, or until the fennel is tender and caramelized.

Rating

Rating: 4/5

Cooking time

Cooking time: 20-25 minutes

Tips

For a sweeter sauce, add more sugar to taste.
For a tangier sauce, add more orange zest to taste.
If the sauce becomes too thick, add a splash of water to thin it out.

Filet Mignon with Truffle Butter

Ingredients

Filet mignon
Truffle butter

Instruction

1. Remove the filet mignon from the refrigerator and let it come to room temperature for about 30 minutes.
2. Preheat a cast iron skillet or grill pan over medium-high heat.
3. Season the filet mignon with salt and pepper to taste.
4. Sear the filet mignon in the hot skillet for 2-3 minutes per side, or until golden brown.
5. Reduce the heat to medium and add the truffle butter to the skillet. Baste the filet mignon with the melted truffle butter and cook to desired doneness.

Rating

Rating: 5/5

Cooking time

Cooking time: 2-3 minutes per side

Tips

Use cold ingredients. The cold butter will create pockets of steam when it bakes, giving the biscuits a light and fluffy texture.

Work the butter into the flour until it resembles coarse crumbs. Overworking the butter will make the biscuits tough.

Knead the dough gently until just combined. Overkneading will develop the gluten, making the biscuits tough.

Pomegranate Glazed Chicken Thighs

Ingredients

Boneless, skinless chicken thighs
Pomegranate juice
Olive oil
Honey
Dijon mustard
Garlic powder
Onion powder
Salt
Pepper

Instruction

1. In a bowl, combine pomegranate juice, olive oil, honey, Dijon mustard, garlic powder, onion powder, salt, and pepper.
2. Add chicken thighs to the bowl and turn to coat.
3. Cover and refrigerate for at least 30 minutes, or up to overnight.
4. Preheat oven to 400°F (200°C).
5. Bake chicken for 20-25 minutes, or until cooked through and glaze is set.

Rating

Rating: 4/5

Cooking time

Cooking time: 20-25 minutes

Tips

Brown the Sausage: Be sure to cook the sausage until it's fully browned for a more flavorful stuffing.

Sauté the Veggies: Don't skip sautéing the onion and celery until softened to bring out their sweetness.

Heat Through: Cook the stuffing until it's heated through, ensuring that all the ingredients are cooked and the flavors have blended.

Beet and Goat Cheese Salad

Ingredients

Beets
Goat cheese
Walnuts
Arugula
Honey
Olive oil
Salt
Pepper

Instruction

1. Roast beets until tender and dice them into bite-sized pieces.
2. Crumble goat cheese into small pieces.
3. Toss arugula with olive oil, salt, and pepper.
4. Arrange beets, goat cheese, walnuts, and arugula on a platter.
5. Drizzle honey over the salad and serve immediately.

Rating

Rating: 4/5

Cooking time

Cooking time: 20 minutes

Tips

For a richer flavor, use heavy cream instead of milk.
Add a pinch of nutmeg or cayenne pepper for a kick of spice.
Serve Creamed Spinach as a side dish with grilled or roasted meat or fish.

Stuffed Lobster with Crab and Parmesan

Ingredients

Lobster tails
Crab meat
Breadcrumbs
Parmesan cheese
Butter
Garlic
Shallots
Herbs
Salt and pepper

Instruction

1. Remove lobster meat from the shells and chop into bite-sized pieces.
2. Combine crab meat, breadcrumbs, Parmesan cheese, butter, garlic, shallots, herbs, salt, and pepper in a bowl.
3. Stuff the lobster shells with the crab mixture.
4. Place stuffed lobster shells on a baking sheet and bake at 375°F (190°C) for 15-20 minutes, or until the lobster meat is cooked through.
5. Serve with melted butter or your favorite sauce.

Rating

Rating: 4/5

Cooking time

Cooking time: 15-20 minutes

Tips

Choose fresh, firm Brussels sprouts. Avoid any that are wilted or have brown spots.

Preheat your oven to 400°F (200°C) before tossing the sprouts with olive oil, maple syrup, salt, and pepper. This will help them caramelize and brown evenly. Spread the sprouts evenly on a baking sheet and roast for 15-20 minutes, or until tender and slightly browned. Don't overcrowd the pan, or they will steam instead of roast.

Citrus Herb Roasted Chicken

Ingredients

Whole chicken
Lemons
Oranges
Fresh thyme
Fresh rosemary
Olive oil
Salt and pepper

Instruction

1. Preheat oven to 400°F (200°C).
2. Remove chicken from refrigerator and bring to room temperature for 30 minutes.
3. Season chicken with salt and pepper.
4. Cut lemons and oranges into wedges and place inside the chicken cavity along with thyme and rosemary.
5. Drizzle with olive oil and roast for 1 hour, or until chicken reaches an internal temperature of 165°F (74°C).

Rating

Rating: 4/5

Cooking time

Cooking time: 1 hour

Tips

For a richer flavor, use a combination of mushrooms such as oyster, cremini, and shiitake.
Add a squeeze of lemon juice to the filling for a tangy twist.
Top the mushrooms with extra Parmesan cheese before baking for a crispy topping.

Chocolate Fondue with Fresh Fruit

Ingredients

Dark chocolate
Heavy cream
Vanilla extract
Fresh fruit (strawberries, bananas, apples, etc.)

Instruction

1. Melt the dark chocolate in a double boiler or in the microwave in 30-second intervals, stirring in between, until smooth.
2. Stir in the heavy cream and vanilla extract until well combined.
3. Pour the fondue into a small serving dish and keep warm over a candle warmer or in a fondue pot.
4. Arrange the fresh fruit on a plate or skewers for dipping.
5. Enjoy the chocolate fondue with your favorite fruits!

Rating

Rating: 4.5/5

Cooking time

Cooking time: 10 minutes

Tips

Wash 3 types of greens and spin dry.
Thinly slice 2 apples and 1/2 red onion.
Toast 1 cup pecans in the oven at 350 degrees for 5-7 minutes.

Classic Beef Bourguignon

Ingredients

Beef chuck roast
Bacon
Carrots
Onions
Mushrooms
Garlic
Flour
Beef broth
Burgundy wine
Thyme
Bay leaf
Salt
Pepper

Instruction

1. Season beef and brown in bacon fat. Remove and set aside.
2. Sauté carrots, onions, and mushrooms. Add garlic and cook for 1 minute.
3. Sprinkle flour over vegetables and cook for 1 minute. Add broth and wine.
4. Return beef to the pot and add thyme, bay leaf, salt, and pepper.
5. Simmer for 2-3 hours, or until beef is tender.

Rating

Rating: 4/5

Cooking time

Cooking time: 2-3 hours

Tips

For the best flavor, use fresh, tender kale. Massage the dressing into the kale for at least 15 minutes to allow the flavors to meld. This salad can be served immediately or chilled for later.

Asparagus and Prosciutto Bundles

Ingredients

Asparagus
Prosciutto
Parmesan
Olive oil
Lemon juice
Salt and pepper

Instruction

1. Preheat oven to 400°F (200°C).
2. Wrap 1 asparagus spear with 1 prosciutto slice and sprinkle with grated Parmesan cheese.
3. Repeat steps 2 for all asparagus spears and place bundles on a baking sheet.
4. Drizzle with olive oil, lemon juice, salt, and pepper.
5. Bake for 10-12 minutes or until the prosciutto is crispy and the asparagus is tender.

Rating

Rating: 4.5/5

Cooking time

Cooking time: 10-12 minutes

Tips

Use fresh Romaine lettuce for the best flavor and texture.
Don't overdress the salad, or it will become soggy.
Add croutons and Parmesan cheese to taste.

Miso-Glazed Eggplant with Sesame

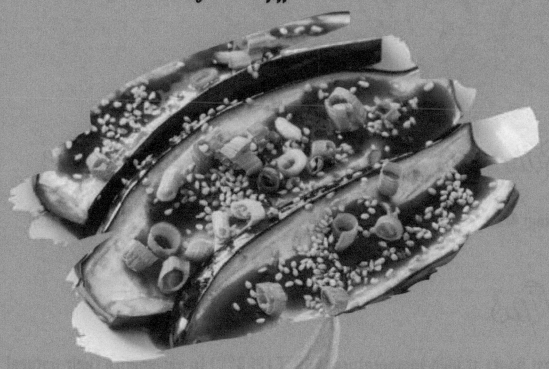

Ingredients

Eggplant
Miso paste
Mirin
Sake
Sugar
Soy sauce
Sesame seeds
Green onions

Instruction

1. Combine miso paste, mirin, sake, sugar, and soy sauce in a small bowl.
2. Cut eggplant into 1/2-inch thick slices and brush with the miso glaze.
3. Grill or pan-fry the eggplant slices until tender and slightly charred.
4. Sprinkle with sesame seeds and green onions.
5. Serve immediately.

Rating

Rating: 4/5

Cooking time

Cooking time: 15-20 minutes

Tips

Roast beets at high temperature: 400°F (200°C) to caramelize their natural sweetness.
Allow beets to cool before handling: This prevents the hot beets from staining your hands or clothes.
Toss salad gently: To avoid breaking up the tender beets and goat cheese.

Pumpkin Sage Gnocchi with Brown Butter

Ingredients

Pumpkin puree
Allpurpose flour
Nutmeg
Sage
Brown butter
ParmigianoReggiano cheese

Instruction

1. Combine pumpkin puree, flour, and nutmeg in a large bowl.
2. Form into bite-sized gnocchi.
3. Pan-fry in melted brown butter until golden brown.
4. Add chopped sage and cook until fragrant.
5. Top with grated Parmigiano-Reggiano cheese and serve immediately.

Rating

Rating: 4/5

Cooking time

Cooking time: 15 minutes

Tips

For a sweeter salad, add more dried cranberries or raisins.
For a nuttier flavor, toast the pecans before adding them to the salad.
For a more tangy flavor, add more lemon juice or feta cheese.

Grilled Shrimp Skewers with Chimichurri

Ingredients

Shrimp
Olive oil
Lemon juice
Garlic
Oregano
Parsley
Cilantro
Red onion
Red wine vinegar
Salt
Pepper

Instruction

1. Devein and season shrimp with salt and pepper.
2. Create skewers by alternating shrimp and red onion slices.
3. Brush skewers with olive oil.
4. Grill skewers for 2-3 minutes per side, or until shrimp are cooked through.
5. Serve with chimichurri made by combining lemon juice, garlic, oregano, parsley, cilantro, red wine vinegar, salt, and pepper.

Rating

Rating: 5/5

Cooking time

Cooking time: 2-3 minutes per side

Tips

Three essential ingredients: apples, walnuts, and lettuce.
Two simple steps: combine and dress.
One delightful salad: ready to enjoy.

Roasted Rack of Lamb with Mint Pesto

Ingredients

Rack of lamb
Olive oil
Salt
Pepper
Mint
Basil
Pine nuts
Parmesan cheese
Garlic
Lemon juice

Instruction

1. Season the rack of lamb with salt, pepper, and olive oil. Roast at 400°F (200°C) for 25-30 minutes, or until cooked to your desired doneness.
2. While the lamb is roasting, prepare the mint pesto by combining mint, basil, pine nuts, Parmesan cheese, garlic, lemon juice, and olive oil in a blender or food processor until smooth.
3. Remove the lamb from the oven and let it rest for 10 minutes before slicing.
4. Spread the mint pesto over the sliced lamb and serve.
5. Enjoy!

Rating

Rating: 5/5

Cooking time

Cooking time: 35-40 minutes

Tips

Shred the cabbage and carrots into a large bowl for easy mixing.
Whisk together the dressing ingredients in a separate bowl to ensure a smooth and well-combined mixture.
Refrigerate the slaw for at least 30 minutes before serving to allow the flavors to blend, resulting in a more flavorful dish.

Truffle Mac and Cheese

Ingredients

Medium shells pasta
Heavy cream
Parmesan cheese
Truffle oil
Truffle butter
Salt
Pepper

Instruction

1. Cook the pasta according to the package directions.
2. In a large saucepan, melt the truffle butter over medium heat.
3. Whisk in the heavy cream and bring to a simmer.
4. Add the Parmesan cheese, salt, and pepper to taste.
5. Stir in the cooked pasta and truffle oil.

Rating

Rating: 5/5

Cooking time

Cooking time: 20 mins

Tips

Cook the bacon first. This will give the bacon fat a chance to flavor the eggs and spinach.

Fry the eggs over medium heat. This will help them to cook evenly without burning.

Season the salad to taste. Salt and pepper are essential, but you can also add other spices like garlic powder or onion powder.

Seared Tuna with Wasabi Cream

Ingredients

Seared Tuna
Wasabi Cream

Instruction

1. Sear tuna steaks in a pan until cooked to desired doneness.
2. While the tuna is searing, whisk together wasabi, soy sauce, and mayonnaise to create the wasabi cream.
3. Remove the tuna from the pan and let it rest for a few minutes.
4. Place the tuna on a plate and top with the wasabi cream.
5. Serve immediately.

Rating

Rating: 4/5

Cooking time

Cooking time: 10 minutes

Tips

For a flavorful twist, use tri-color penne pasta.
Add grilled chicken or shrimp for a protein boost.
Top with a sprinkle of fresh basil or parsley for extra freshness.

Elegant Baked Salmon with Dill Sauce

Ingredients

Salmon fillet
Olive oil
Salt
Pepper
Lemon slices
Dill sprigs
Dill Sauce
Sour cream
Mayonnaise
Fresh dill
Lemon juice
Salt
Pepper

Instruction

1. Season salmon with olive oil, salt, and pepper. Top with lemon slices and dill sprigs.
2. Bake at 400°F (200°C) for 15-20 minutes, or until cooked through.
3. While salmon bakes, whisk together sour cream, mayonnaise, dill, lemon juice, salt, and pepper for the dill sauce.
4. Spread dill sauce over baked salmon.
5. Serve immediately with lemon wedges or additional dill garnish.

Rating

Rating: 4/5

Cooking time

Cooking time: 15-20 minutes

Tips

Add feta cheese for creaminess
Red onion adds a bit of sharpness 3.Fresh parsley brings a light freshness to the salad

Lentil and Mushroom Shepherd's Pie

Ingredients

Lentils
Mushrooms
Onion
Garlic
Carrots
Celery
Vegetable broth
Tomato paste
Herbs and spices
Mashed potatoes

Instruction

1. Cook lentils according to package directions.
2. Sauté mushrooms, onion, garlic, carrots, and celery in a skillet.
3. Stir in tomato paste, vegetable broth, herbs, and spices.
4. Spread lentil mixture in a baking dish.
5. Top with mashed potatoes and bake until potatoes are golden brown.

Rating

Rating: 4/5

Cooking time

Cooking time: 1 hour

Tips

Create a flaky crust by using cold ingredients and working the dough as little as possible.

For a perfectly smooth filling, blend the pumpkin mixture until it is lump-free.

Don't overbake the pie! It is done when a knife inserted into the center comes out clean.

Creamy Garlic Mashed Potatoes with Chives

Ingredients

Russet potatoes
Garlic cloves
Butter
Whole milk
Sour cream
Chives

Instruction

1. Peel and cut potatoes into chunks. Boil until tender.
2. While potatoes boil, mince garlic and sauté in butter.
3. Drain potatoes, mash, and add sautéed garlic, milk, sour cream, salt, and pepper.
4. Mash until smooth and creamy, adding more milk if needed.
5. Top with chopped chives for garnish.

Rating

Rating: 4.5/5

Cooking time

Cooking time: 30 minutes

Tips

Preheat the oven to the correct temperature before starting to make the pie. Chill the dough for at least 30 minutes before rolling it out. This will help prevent the dough from shrinking and becoming tough.
Brush the edges of the crust with egg wash before baking to help it brown and stay crisp.

Twice-Baked Potatoes with Gruyère

Ingredients

Potatoes
Gruyère cheese
Heavy cream
Butter
Salt
Pepper

Instruction

1. Bake potatoes until tender; cut in half lengthwise, scoop out flesh.
2. Mash potato flesh with Gruyère, cream, butter, salt, and pepper.
3. Fill potato skins with mixture; top with more Gruyère.
4. Bake at 375°F (190°C) until heated through and golden brown.
5. Serve hot.

Rating

Rating: 5/5

Cooking time

Cooking time: 1 hour

Tips

Use a variety of apples for a complex flavor.
Don't overmix the topping, or it will become tough.
Bake the crisp until the topping is golden brown and the apples are tender.

Pistachio-Crusted Salmon with Honey Glaze

Ingredients

Salmon fillets
Pistachios, finely ground
Honey
Olive oil
Lemon juice
Garlic cloves, minced
Dijon mustard
Salt and pepper

Instruction

1. Preheat oven to 400°F (200°C).
2. In a shallow dish, combine ground pistachios, honey, olive oil, lemon juice, garlic, Dijon mustard, salt, and pepper.
3. Dip salmon fillets into the mixture, coating evenly.
4. Place salmon on a greased baking sheet.
5. Bake for 15-20 minutes, or until cooked through and golden brown.

Rating

Rating: 5/5

Cooking time

Cooking time: 15-20 minutes

Tips

Preheat oven to 350°F (175°C).
Beat cream cheese and sugar until fluffy.
Cook and stir caramel drizzle until thickened.

Elegant Holiday Cheese Board

Ingredients

Brie
Camembert
Blue cheese
Cheddar
Gouda
Fruit (such as grapes, apples, and pears)
Nuts (such as almonds, walnuts, and pecans)
Crackers
Honey

Instruction

1. Arrange the cheeses on a platter, with Brie and Camembert as the focal points.
2. Fill in the spaces with the remaining cheeses, creating a colorful and visually appealing display.
3. Scatter the fruit around the cheeses, providing a sweet and refreshing contrast.
4. Sprinkle the nuts over the platter, adding texture and crunch.
5. Place the crackers and honey in small bowls or ramekins alongside the cheese board for easy serving.

Rating

Rating: 4/5

Cooking time

Cooking time: 0 minutes

Tips

Use a good quality butter. The butter is what gives the pie its rich flavor, so don't skimp on the quality.

Don't overmix the dough. Overmixing will make the pie tough. Just mix until the ingredients are combined.

Let the pie cool completely before slicing and serving. This will help the pie set and prevent it from falling apart.

Zucchini Noodles with Pesto and Cherry Tomatoes

Ingredients

zucchini
spiralizer
pesto
cherry tomatoes
olive oil
salt
pepper

Instruction

1. Spiralize zucchini into noodles.
2. Heat olive oil in a pan and sauté cherry tomatoes.
3. Add zucchini noodles to the pan and cook until tender.
4. Stir in pesto, salt, and pepper.
5. Serve immediately.

Rating

Rating: 5/5

Cooking time

Cooking time: 15 minutes

Tips

Knead the dough thoroughly to develop elasticity.
Let the rolls rise in a warm place for maximum fluffiness.
Frost the rolls with a generous amount of cream cheese frosting.

Savory Sweet Potato Galette

Ingredients

Sweet potatoes
Olive oil
Salt
Black pepper
Thyme
Garlic
Onion
Brie cheese
Parmesan cheese
Eggs
Milk
Pie crust

Instruction

1. Preheat oven to 400°F (200°C). Peel and slice sweet potatoes thinly.
2. In a large bowl, toss sweet potatoes with olive oil, salt, pepper, thyme, garlic, and onion.
3. Spread sweet potato mixture evenly over a pie crust in a pie plate. Top with brie cheese and Parmesan cheese.
4. In a separate bowl, whisk together eggs, milk, salt, and pepper. Pour over sweet potato mixture.
5. Bake for 30-35 minutes, or until sweet potatoes are tender and eggs are set.

Rating

Rating: 4/5

Cooking time

Cooking time: 30-35 minutes

Tips

Spice it up: Don't be shy with the spices! Cinnamon, nutmeg, and ginger add depth of flavor to the pie filling.

Use a graham cracker crust: A graham cracker crust provides a sweet and crunchy base for the pie.

Make it ahead: This pie can be made ahead of time and refrigerated for up to 2 days before baking.

Chocolate Hazelnut Torte

Ingredients

Flour
Sugar
Butter
Eggs
Chocolate
Hazelnuts
Rum
Espresso

Instruction

1. In a bowl, combine flour, sugar, and butter.
2. In a separate bowl, whisk eggs, chocolate, hazelnuts, rum, and espresso.
3. Add the wet ingredients to the dry ingredients and mix until just combined.
4. Pour the batter into a greased and floured cake pan.
5. Bake at 350°F (175°C) for 30-35 minutes, or until a toothpick inserted into the center comes out clean.

Rating

Rating: 4/5

Cooking time

Cooking time: 30-35 minutes

Tips

Preheat oven to 350°F (175°C).
Combine cranberries, apples, sugar, and cinnamon in a baking dish.
In a separate bowl, mix oats, flour, brown sugar, and butter until crumbly.

Classic French Onion Soup

Ingredients

Beef broth
Onions
Butter
Sugar
Flour
Bay leaf
Thyme
Salt
Pepper
Gruyère cheese
Baguette

Instruction

1. Caramelize onions in butter with sugar until deep golden brown.
2. Deglaze the pan with beef broth and add bay leaf and thyme.
3. Simmer for at least 30 minutes or up to several hours.
4. Season to taste with salt and pepper.
5. Top with Gruyère cheese and toasted baguette slices.

Rating

Rating: 4/5

Cooking time

Cooking time: At least 30 minutes or up to several hours

Tips

Use fresh ginger: Ground ginger loses its flavor over time, so use fresh ginger for the best taste.

Don't overmix the dough: Overmixing the dough will make the cookies tough. Mix just until the ingredients are combined.

Let the cookies cool before icing: If you ice the cookies while they're still warm, the icing will melt and run. Let the cookies cool completely before icing them.

Vanilla Bean Panna Cotta with Berry Compote

Ingredients

Gelatin
Heavy cream
Whole milk
Sugar
Vanilla bean, split and scraped
Berries (strawberries, blueberries, raspberries)
Sugar
Lemon juice

Instruction

1. In a saucepan, whisk together gelatin, heavy cream, milk, sugar, and scraped vanilla bean seeds.
2. Bring to a simmer over medium heat, stirring constantly.
3. Remove from heat and pour into individual serving glasses.
4. Refrigerate for at least 4 hours or overnight.
5. Make the berry compote: In a saucepan, combine berries, sugar, and lemon juice. Bring to a boil over medium heat, then reduce heat and simmer for 10 minutes, or until thickened.

Rating

Rating: 4/5

Cooking time

Cooking time: 10 minutes

Tips

3 ingredients (sugar, corn syrup, chocolate chips) are combined in a large bowl.
3 ingredients (eggs, salt, pecans) are stirred into the filling.
Pie bakes for 50-60 minutes.

Pear and Almond Tart

Ingredients

Shortcrust pastry
Caster sugar
Plain flour
Butter
Pears
Ground almonds
Milk
Eggs
Cinnamon
Vanilla extract
Icing sugar

Instruction

1. Preheat oven to 375°F (190°C).
2. Roll out shortcrust pastry and line a tart tin.
3. Combine caster sugar, flour, butter, ground almonds, milk, eggs, cinnamon, and vanilla extract to create the filling.
4. Peel and thinly slice the pears, then arrange them over the pastry.
5. Pour the filling over the pears and bake for 30-35 minutes, or until golden brown.

Rating

Rating: 4/5

Cooking time

Cooking time: 30-35 minutes

Tips

Combine 3 liquids: apple cider, red wine, and brandy.
Add 3 sliced fruits: orange, lemon, and apple.
Refrigerate for at least 4 hours or overnight.

Decadent Chocolate Lava Cake

Ingredients

Dark chocolate
Butter
Flour
Sugar
Eggs
Vanilla extract

Instruction

1. Preheat oven to 400°F (200°C). Grease and flour individual ramekins or muffin cups.
2. Melt chocolate and butter together in a heatproof bowl over simmering water, stirring until smooth.
3. In a separate bowl, whisk together flour and sugar. Add eggs one at a time, whisking well after each addition.
4. Stir in melted chocolate mixture and vanilla extract. Divide batter evenly between prepared ramekins.
5. Bake for 10-12 minutes, or until a toothpick inserted into the center comes out with just a few moist crumbs attached.

Rating

Rating: 5/5

Cooking time

Cooking time: 10-12 minutes

Tips

For a stronger latte, use double espresso.
For a sweeter latte, add more caramel sauce.
For a richer latte, use full-fat milk.

Cinnamon Sugar Crêpes with Berries

Ingredients

Allpurpose flour
Granulated sugar
Salt
Eggs
Milk
Vanilla extract
Cinnamon
Ground cinnamon
Granulated sugar
Berries

Instruction

1. In a bowl, whisk together flour, sugar, and salt.
2. In a separate bowl, whisk together eggs, milk, and vanilla extract.
3. Gradually whisk wet ingredients into dry ingredients until just combined.
4. Let batter rest for 15 minutes.
5. Heat a lightly oiled skillet over medium heat and cook 1/4 cup batter per crêpe. Sprinkle with cinnamon sugar and berries.

Rating

Rating: 5/5

Cooking time

Cooking time: 15 minutes

Tips

Combine 2 juices
Add 3 spices to steep
Top with 1 fizzy drink

Mango and Passion Fruit Mousse

Ingredients

Mango puree
Passion fruit puree
Heavy cream
Sugar
Gelatin
Lemon juice

Instruction

1. In a bowl, whisk together mango puree, passion fruit puree, sugar, and lemon juice.
2. In a separate bowl, whip heavy cream until stiff peaks form.
3. Sprinkle gelatin over 1/4 cup of water and let bloom for 5 minutes. Heat the bloomed gelatin in the microwave for 15 seconds or until dissolved.
4. Stir the dissolved gelatin into the mango mixture.
5. Fold the whipped cream into the mango mixture. Refrigerate for at least 4 hours or until set.

Rating

Rating: 4/5

Cooking time

Cooking time: 5 minutes

Tips

Use high-quality cocoa powder for a rich and flavorful taste.
Don't oversweeten the hot chocolate add sugar gradually to taste.
Top with a dollop of whipped cream for an extra-indulgent treat.

Cheesecake with Gingersnap Crust

Ingredients

Gingersnap cookies
Butter
Sugar
Cream cheese
Sugar
Sour cream
Vanilla extract
Eggs
Heavy cream

Instruction

1. Preheat oven to 350°F (175°C).
2. Crush gingersnap cookies and mix with melted butter. Press into the bottom of a greased 9-inch springform pan.
3. Beat cream cheese, sugar, and sour cream until smooth. Mix in vanilla extract and eggs.
4. Pour the cheesecake filling over the crust and bake for 45-50 minutes, or until set.
5. Let cool before serving, optionally top with whipped cream or fresh fruit.

Rating

Rating: 5/5

Cooking time

Cooking time: 45-50 minutes

Tips

Use high-quality unsweetened sparkling pear juice for the best flavor.
Add ginger liqueur to taste, depending on how strong you want the drink to be.
Garnish with fresh pear slices for a refreshing touch.

Spiced Orange and Cranberry Compote

Ingredients

12 Cranberries
3 Oranges
1/4 cup brown sugar
1/2 teaspoon grated fresh ginger
1/4 teaspoon ground allspice
1/8 teaspoon ground cinnamon

Instruction

1. Zest and juice 2 oranges; segment the remaining orange.
2. Combine cranberries, orange segments, sugar, ginger, allspice, cinnamon, and orange juice in a small saucepan.
3. Bring to a simmer over medium heat, stirring often.
4. Reduce heat to low and simmer until cranberries burst and mixture thickens, about 15 minutes.
5. Remove from heat and stir in orange zest.

Rating

Rating: 4/5

Cooking time

Cooking time: 15 minutes

Tips

Shake well for 10-15 seconds to ensure the ingredients are fully combined and chilled.
Use fresh ice to keep your drink cold and prevent it from becoming diluted.
Garnish with a lemon wedge or orange peel for a refreshing and aromatic touch.

Maple Glazed Brussels Sprouts

Ingredients

Maple syrup
Olive oil
Brussels sprouts
Salt and pepper

Instruction

1. Preheat oven to 400°F (200°C).
2. Toss Brussels sprouts with olive oil, salt, and pepper.
3. Spread sprouts on a baking sheet and roast for 20-25 minutes, or until tender and slightly browned.
4. In a small saucepan, heat maple syrup until it simmers.
5. Remove sprouts from the oven and toss with the maple syrup glaze.

Rating

Rating: 4/5

Cooking time

Cooking time: 20-25 minutes

Tips

Combine all ingredients in a large pot.
Heat over medium heat until hot and fragrant.
Reduce heat to low and simmer for at least 30 minutes.

Seared Duck Breast with Pomegranate Sauce

Ingredients

Duck breasts
Pomegranate seeds
Red onion
Garlic
Ginger
Honey
Soy sauce
Rice vinegar
Sesame oil

Instruction

1. Score the duck breast skin and sear in a hot pan.
2. Cook the duck breasts in a preheated oven until desired doneness.
3. In a bowl, combine pomegranate seeds, red onion, garlic, ginger, honey, soy sauce, rice vinegar, and sesame oil.
4. Bring the sauce to a boil, then reduce heat and simmer until thickened.
5. Serve the seared duck breast with the pomegranate sauce.

Rating

Rating: 4.5/5

Cooking time

Cooking time: 25 minutes

Tips

Sweeten to taste: Adjust the amount of cinnamon syrup based on your desired sweetness level.

Use fresh spices: Ground cinnamon provides a more aromatic and flavorful touch than pre-ground cinnamon.

Layer it up: Add the whipped cream and cinnamon topping last for a visually appealing and flavorful presentation.

Savory Mushroom and Spinach Quiche

Ingredients

Puff pastry
Eggs
Heavy cream
Milk
Salt
Pepper
Mushrooms
Spinach
Onion
Garlic
Butter
Parmesan cheese

Instruction

1. Preheat oven to 375°F (190°C).
2. Sauté mushrooms, spinach, onion, and garlic in butter until softened.
3. Whisk together eggs, cream, milk, salt, and pepper.
4. Roll out puff pastry and place in a 9-inch pie plate.
5. Layer sautéed mixture and Parmesan cheese into the pastry, then pour in egg mixture.

Rating

Rating: 4.5/5

Cooking time

Cooking time: 30-35 minutes

Tips

Add a dash of ground nutmeg for a hint of spice.
Serve chilled over ice for a refreshing treat.
Garnish with apple slices or cinnamon sticks for a festive touch.

Caramelized Apple Tart Tatin

Ingredients

Sugar
Butter
Apples
Puff pastry

Instruction

1. Melt sugar and butter in a skillet until caramelized.
2. Arrange apple slices over the caramel.
3. Roll out puff pastry and place it over the apples.
4. Trim the edges of the puff pastry.
5. Bake at 400°F (200°C) for 30-35 minutes, or until the pastry is golden brown.

Rating

Rating: 5/5

Cooking time

Cooking time: 30-35 minutes

Tips

Steep loose herbal tea in hot water.
Add fresh mint leaves and honey.
Cool and pour over ice.

Acknowledgment

I am truly grateful to my family and friends for their endless support and encouragement as I developed these recipes. To the culinary mentors and inspirations in my life, thank you for teaching me the beauty of elegant cooking. And to you, the reader, thank you for letting this book be a part of your holiday traditions. May your celebrations be filled with joy, love, and beautiful flavors.

---Margaret N. Brown---

Made in United States
Orlando, FL
24 November 2024

54362450R00070